Double Bind

Double Bind

Leslie Howard

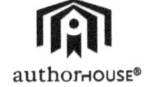

authorHOUSE®

AuthorHouse™
1663 Liberty Drive
Bloomington, IN 47403
www.authorhouse.com
Phone: 1-800-839-8640

First published by AuthorHouse   07/05/2011

ISBN: 978-1-4567-8565-9 (sc)
ISBN: 978-1-4567-8564-2 (ebk)

Printed in the United States of America

Any people depicted in stock imagery provided by Thinkstock are models, and such images are being used for illustrative purposes only. Certain stock imagery © Thinkstock.

This book is printed on acid-free paper.

Introduction

I have no doubt that Childline and other such like have done a lot of good to a lot of children. However when children are used by parents and grandparents to express their own clear, simple and obvious personal grudge then the question becomes who is the abuser and who becomes the abused?

The following constitutes the basis of a complaint about my mental condition I made to Liverpools' Chief Constable back in August 2004. It is now June 2012 and I am still awaiting any rational response. The article outlines my "mental illness" and what caused it.

It contains some very private and personal information. However public interest issues mean that if the following can help others get their schizophrenia or depression into some kind of perspective then publication is justified. It is intended for sufferers, carers and the medical profession, and may offer a different if not unusual light on depression or schizophrenia in general. It may seem long-winded and go into some detail but the conclusions and issues raised apply universally to any stress related condition e.g. epilepsy. No matter what, it constitutes an interesting intellectual exercise.

It all started when I moved to GEC Plessey Telecommunications Ltd at Edge Lane Liverpool in 1989. I started to work there as an electronics engineer in the Microelectronics Centre performing electronics component qualification and test working under Brian Stewart in the digital components side of the department under Department Head Alan Garner. I got burgled and a number of factors incriminated the landlord and his family. At the time I was in Tony's B&B on Edge lane. I won't go into details about the burglary because they are now irrelevant. I told a person who I believe is called Alan Johnson who was working and living in the same place as me about my concerns. Instead of taking it as a friendly warning, comment was "You have insulted people who are good friends of mine and I'm not going to let you get away with it ". The following day he was talking in the canteen with John Heywood who first interviewed me when I arrived in Liverpool. I don't know what was said but from the expression on John Heywoods face it was rather good. His jaw dropped, his eyes opened wide and he looked shocked.

"Are you willing to make this a formal charge?" he asked.

"Yes" came the reply, stroking his moustache. I wondered what he said.

Alan then left for Gibralta to do an installation there, obviously hoping I wasn't going to be around when he came back. The answer to this formal charge came the following Monday. John Heywood was talking to a couple of people who I took as company directors. John Heywood pointed me out over the canteen table.

"That man, Alan says that he masturbates in his room".

One of the directors nearly spat out his peas.

John continued "In front of young children!. If what Alan says is true then what a horrible man" contorting his face in disgust.

"Sack him" said the director.

"I agree. How do you want to go about it?"

"First leak that Alan says that he masturbates. What else have you got on him?" "He lied. He got his cousin's son the sack"

"Leak that he did it deliberately. What did the police say?"

"No evidence" said John.

"Do they think he knew they were there?"

"They think he did"

"Did they see anything?", asked the director.

"No"

What I believe they saw when they opened the door was me standing at the sink fully clothed with my back to them for what I later found out was five minutes. They didn't see anything, say anything, or do anything. For all I know or the family know I might have been brushing my teeth, picking my nose squeezing zits or washing myself. There never was any hot water in that place for a hot bath. What I believe started as a joke between the family and the other guests over the breakfast table turned out to be an excuse to cause trouble for me.

There are a number of reasons why I came to this conclusion.

Firstly something was wrong (I think). Something wasn't quite right but the only thing I could feel was ill at ease.

Secondly the bedroom door was open. I was sure I'd locked it.

Expert medical opinion who knows me extremely well took one look at the at the above and immediately concluded that my mind had been distorted. Probably.

I was paying my rent one day and the landlady said in pidgin English

"Tony, he's da man dat mas I roo (He's the man that masturbates in his room).

I turned red, made my excuses and left.

Finally the landlady's children were laughing hysterically outside my door. "Come out with your hands up ", they shouted. I finally realised what their joke was and was physically and violently sick in the toilet. How these charges came about I to this day do not know. Was it through a joke I had with Alan the previous night about the shape of the male part? Namely why it has a bell-end. I got my Degree at Imperial College London. Imperial consisted of three colleges at the time: the Royal School of Mines, The Royal College of Science, and City and Guilds. There was a big debate amongst us lesser intellectuals about the shape of the male part, namely the "bell-end".

The Royal School of Mines experimented for a month and came to the conclusion that the bell-end is for the male pleasure.

The Royal College of Science experimented for two months and came to the conclusion that the bell-end is for the female pleasure.

City & Guilds, my college we experimented vociferously for six months and came to the unanimous conclusion that the bell-end was to stop your hand falling off the end.

This blokes' very next sentence was "When are you going to leave GPT?" It could have been as simple as that.

Weeks earlier Alan Johnson went to John Heywood (personnel) in the canteen to make a complaint about me. He complained that I'd been given the sack from a previous job and this wasn't included in my c.v. Comment from John Heywood was "Well we knew there was something wrong but we won't be too worried about that". Alan certainly had it in for me.

If anything did happen why wasn't I confronted? Why did the family wait for weeks to call in the police? If, as they claimed I was a threat to their children why wasn't I kicked out on the streets? All of a sudden the families joke was no longer funny. I had decided to leave GPT Liverpool but was going to leave the house and the company on my own terms. After the incident when I realised what the families joke was for the next few months I used Liverpool as a vomitorium. Things got worse. One day Ray Ellis was talking to Gordon Nelson who worked alongside him "Alan says that he masturbates" "He doesn't like him then", came the reply. At about the same time my boss Brian Stewart was talking to John Moss, a workmate one morning "They've found a number of other character problems which they're getting quite concerned about".

When I was working as a lecturer in my home town my cousins' son was planning on leaving his job to join the RAF. When confronted about this I said I didn't know anything about it. I lied, got found out, and suffered. Over the next few days I was pointed out by John Heywood over the canteen table "Alan says that he masturbates." said John "Pass it on." I stopped using the canteen.

Brian my boss was talking to John Moss one morning "They're scared in case he finds out what Alan says about him"

"Why?" asked John.

"Because they're scared in case he might leave".

I already had a good idea what Alan said about me. The next thing I remember is Brian talking to John again "They've found a number of body fluids (coming out of the sink) and they're getting quite concerned about his health. They're thinking about calling in a doctor".

The body fluids they got were lots of vomit and bile, mucous, saliva, pus, phlegm and possibly urine. No semen.

One day Brian was again talking to John "They searched his room and found other incriminating evidence." I was later looking through my laundry bag and found a pair of my mothers tights and my kid sisters knickers. Incriminating evidence?. I wondered. My mother had done my packing for me. One day a couple of people I worked with were talking in the test area. One turned to the other and asked

"Why would he deliberately get his cousin the sack from his first ever job?"

Nissan? I wondered.

"His cousins son"

"His cousins son then. Why would he then lie about it?."

My cousins son?

I don't know."

After this I started masturbating in the sink to see what would happen. The solution I thought was to deliberately incriminate myself, try to be confronted and then make counter-charges of slander and conspiracy against the family and personnel. It is however a habit I had for years but I hadn't done anything wrong. I still haven't met a solitary bloke who hasn't tried it. Later I heard Brian "Those samples have started coming now. The trouble is they're contaminated." I later thought my shampoo was a bit sparse. The contaminant?. Later Brian said that they had back-annotated a non-contaminated sample and they matched. Over the next few weeks I believe word got passed round the factory "He does" I was the subject of much hilarity.

I then started getting numerous and frequent proposals from prostitutes. There was always someone in the background. Coincidence? One night I was in the bar across the road to where I lived. A girl told a joke and when I laughed she kicked me in the shins. I had never had such an introduction before. Something was wrong but I couldn't figure out what so I left alone at the end of the night.

One day I was walking into the coffee room and a few of my colleagues were talking "They reckon he only lasted five minutes." "What the way his hand shakes I'm not bloody surprised." "Funny bloody ha-ha" thinks I. But even I had to laugh at that one. One day a girl from a different department walked into the coffee room while I was in "He did it when he was a student." I still can't help wondering "How the hell did they know I used to masturbate as a student?" Guesswork? Or the joke I told Alan that night? Running joke as a student at the time with the rugby team was "First one to fill the bucket wins."

Next came my birthday. I was in the bar of my local The Augustus John when a couple of friends bought me a joke pair of glasses with a penis as a nose. I believed and still believe the idea came from Terry the landlord who had friends in CID. I remember thinking that this was going to get me into even more trouble. At the end of the night after a few drinks I put the glasses on and played with them as the joke they were meant to be. The following day Brian was talking to John Moss indicating a growth on the nose. I thought it was me he was talking about.

The Department Head was off somewhere and his understudy was on holiday so I took Brian into the coffee room and confronted him. He said he hadn't heard anything. But I had heard him mention Alan, the character problems, the incriminating evidence, the samples that were contaminated, the sample that matched and indicating a growth (a penis?) on the nose.

"It's amazing what you can find out by lip-reading personnel over the canteen table" I said.

When Brian left the coffee room he met a colleague

"What's wrong with him?" asked Tim.

"He's just found out what Alan's been saying about him."

After coming from home on holiday I couldn't get a reply from the landlord to get a key to my room. So I moved to a hotel for a few days.

One night after work Brian asked me where I was staying so I told him. He walked off in the direction of Personnel. Later that night I got a knock on my door. When I answered the man said he was after room 11. I thought this was odd. He was too drunk to identify a large number 10 on my door but was sober enough to carry a tray of halves (halves?) up the stairs. Later that night I noticed my door lock was broken. I thought I had been burgled again but nothing was missing. The following morning I got up to go to work and across the street in the window I noticed the shape of two figures in the building opposite. Here again I thought this was odd because the Chinese restaurant wasn't open at the time. On my way to work waiting for the bus across the road I noticed the top floor, second from the right, room number 10, my room was the only one without any net curtains. The curtains were open. I was sure I had shut them the previous night. I was kicked out of one hotel after another and eventually in mid November moved to Borrowdale Road where I stayed for the rest of my time in Liverpool. From here I met John and Ann-Marie. John was a trainee nurse and Ann-Marie was a barmaid and later became a trainee nurse herself.

Terry was in the bar of the Augustus John one night: "Beast" Terry Crewe said in a low voice "Beast". I reasoned that he knew of the allegations made against me. By this time I was depressed and confided in him that I had even considered suicide as a way out of the situation I had found myself in. I was clearly being picked on by the entire personnel department over a period of months.

Word soon got round the Company. I was in the alley at work one day and two men stared at me "Suicide would be the best thing for him." said one "Suicide or prison" came the reply. By this time it was early November 1990.

One night in the Augustus John a few of Terry's mates in CID were talking at the bar. One was practicing arm-locks. "I always thought Geordies were a bunch of wankers." said one. Later a more senior officer arrived "We'll test him" he said "to see if he cracks. Some do, some don't." They were going to pick me up later that evening. Something was wrong. I wasn't ready to be questioned yet so I left by the back exit. After a few days I put things together. The charges, the character problems, the incriminating evidence, the samples, the prostitutes, the joke glasses, the broken door lock and the figures across the road. A set-up. It wasn't just Personnel who were setting me up. It was the investigating officer in CID. Oh shit!

One night I was invited to Ann-Marie's and poured my heart out to her. I told her that I thought I had been caught masturbating in my room and accused of masturbating in front of young children. I had been picked on by Personnel, genetic fingerprint tested, broken into almost daily and was the victim of systematic entrapment by the local CID.

"How do you know this?" she asked.

"Picture fits"

"Perhaps you enjoyed it."

"No." I said firmly, shaking my head.

It's like the sinking of the Belgrano. Two years before the event a John Henty a top dog in the Institute of Actuaries looked at the state of the economy and came to the conclusion that what we needed was a war. "Great for the economy." Two years later the Government received warming of a military build-up in the South Atlantic. They are supposed to have written this on a scrap of paper and lost it. No chance. As far as the sinking is concerned the Belgrano was followed by not one sub but three for a period of days. I got that from a navigator of one of the submarines. If the captain knew the subs were there he would turn home (which he did). If he didn't know they were there how could he pose any threat?. It's not difficult to paint a picture of a war which was deliberately started.

That's the way my mind works. I have been trained in systems which mean I put pieces of a puzzle together and form a reasonable conclusion.

In the coffee room at work a workmate was talking to a Test Machine Operator. All I heard was "All because he has this slightly anti-social habit." My slightly anti-social habit?

I was sitting in the bar of the A.J. one night and a crowd turned up, I believe from Personnel at work and sat around me. One young-looking lad was talking about the charges and evidence against me. He concluded his conversation that it was difficult to stop masturbating at the point of climax and that I had probably only realized that the children were there when it was too late to do anything about it. I was therefore found innocent of the charges against me, that Personnel were going to put things right, and they would get in touch with me to propose a settlement and that they wanted me to leave the Company. Alan had been given the sack.

"Sanctimonious bastards" thinks I. They had put me through Hell and didn't even have the guts to say anything to me personally. Comment was "Nobody embarrasses John Heywood like that and gets away with it." In the background people were talking "His mother wouldn't like to hear what he's been up to." In the corner a young girl was talking to a lad sitting next to her
"Do you masturbate?" she asked
"No" he said.
"I do"

A few days later a stranger in a bar offered to buy me a drink. He explained that he was just given six quid from somebody he never met before "Do you know a magazine called VIZ?"

"Yes."

"Well this magazine painted a picture of a man's door lock and said that he had sex with himself for the last ten years." (they were wrong. It was at least 15-20).

"This highly intelligent man recognized the picture of his house and threatened to take them to court. Got ten grand. Comment from Jonathan Ross was "That's got to be worth four wanks." "Four wanks" and the say-so of people with an obvious grudge was the only evidence against me. I thought about this for a while. Taking the money would mean leaving the Company on their terms. I left the B+B on my terms and was going to leave the Company under the same conditions. It also meant letting the Personnel Department, John Heywood, his mate and the local CID get away with what they'd been up to and free to do the same to someone else. The offer was therefore unacceptable.

By this time it was mid December 1989. I went up to Terry Crewe one night and said "They've offered me ten grand to keep quiet. All I've got to do is commit perjury (by not telling the whole truth) to get it. If I do call in Scotland Yard I'll tell the truth, the whole truth and I'll use their own records to prove it." The following day Ray Ellis was talking to a workmate "He threatened to call in Scotland Yard. They nearly shit themselves. Destroyed all his records including the fact he was put on a charge in the first place." I heard Brian subsequently talking to John Moss

"They've had this high-powered meeting."

"What?. About a pain up the 'arris?"

"Gary Head stormed out."

Later on the same day "Apparently he's shown all the symptoms of being a sadist."

I explained to Ann-Marie that night that Personnel had realized their own hypocricy and had started throwing tantrums so now I could leave. This was about when the trouble really started. Things got a lot worse. I was talking to someone who sometimes got in the Augustus John

"You think you've got a lot on your conscience." he said "I've got lives on my conscience. Mowed them down. Killed them. I had to. It's when you're about 50 it gets to you. I've got real heavyweights in my gang. My gang come from over there (pointing to the local mental hospital). You can be in my gang. You're their golden boy. Don't worry there's nobody in Liverpool who's safer than you."

So that's why I was being followed and watched, or so I thought. I patted him on the shoulder, thanked him and left. At least now I had a team of shrinks from the Royal Hospital on my side determining my innocence.

In the bar of the Willowbank Hotel one night, my new local it was student rag week. A girl was selling kisses at 50p a go. At the end of the night she walked past me and said "I'm not kissing him because he masturbates". I felt gutted, dirty and cheap. Why was the local CID and Personnel still making my life miserable? Even a team of shrinks said I was innocent. The only evidence against me was the say-so of a number of people with a grudge.

I was asked by a female nurse I was sharing the house with what I thought of Liverpool. I said jokingly that there was nothing wrong with Liverpool that an irin gas cloud wouldn't put right. A few days later before she left to go to London she was talking in the kitchen to a male friend of hers, who I overheard from the lounge

"There's bound to be some psychological damage after what he's gone through." So she knew as well.

After a few more nights of misery at the Augustus John and the Willowbank Hotel, I went home for Christmas During the Christmas holiday I was in my local Social Club and someone I know well Norman was talking to a friend of his "Him over there he says that he's in real serious trouble with the police" In fact the police were in real serious trouble with me. Were these rumors going to follow me even to my home turf? This meant I had to go back to Liverpool. After the New Year 1990 I returned back to work. After a few more nights of misery Lord Prior the head of GEC, GPT's parent company, now Marconi sent his secretary to visit the Liverpool site. There he was talking to Alan Garner the Department head at the front of the office "I think he's lip-reading us now. I think he is yeah. Wish we had a few more like him, we haven't laughed so much in years. Pity about what we've got to do to him.". I wasn't lip-reading at all. I overheard the conversation over the length of the office. This started me wondering "What the Hell are they up to now?" Was his visit to give Gary Head the sack? Six months later, I think to the day, Gary Head the Director of Personnel resigned from the Company. It must have been a few years at most before he was due to retire and cost him a fortune in his pension rights. When I later asked my boss Brian Stewart who Gary Head was, he said he'd never heard of him. Yet I had previously heard him mention his name indicating he'd shown "all the symptoms of being a sadist ", and I predicted Gary Head would leave the company six months before the event. In between time my treatment continued. The following sequence of events becomes confused due to time, mental illness medication and a long drunken alcoholic stupor. However to me at least all the following events are true. I was in the Willowbank Hotel one night with John and Ann-Marie during a quiz night. Sitting around me were people on the next table discussing my case. During the course of the conversation a young lad confirmed that "They forced the lock on the door, opened the curtains removed the net curtains and set up a camera in the building opposite. They've got pictures of him naked in his room getting dressed". Again in the Willowbank I was watching two people who I half recognized through a hatchway "All because he masturbates, know what I mean?" I never saw them again. Later another night through the doorway someone was pointing at me talking to someone next to him. "They Know him. He's not a pervert. They know him." I tried to take no notice and continued drinking as normal. Listening to this and the goading I received almost all night every night in my three chosen pubs The Willowbank Hotel, The Augustus John and The Prince William got me even further down. In between being sober and getting drunk I was being goaded. After a while every night it seemed to stop after the people goading me left each pub and left me to ponder over what they were saying. Was I still being picked on by Personnel?. Yes. By the local CID?. Yes. By shrinks? I didn't know. Each time I started to come to the conclusion that I was being picked on by shrinks I was given a psychological boost. I was in the Willowbank Hotel one night with John Ann_Marie and a friend of theirs, another John. He was keen to show me a horoscope. It was an ambiguous horoscope, years old and neither mine nor his. In it under one of the signs it said hold on for a while and you will become rather rich soon. I concluded that this was a message from the shrinks who were trying to help me with a promise to give me the files I needed to force a court case. I wasn't after money particularly but if it was there I'd take it. I had a grudge and was after revenge. My treatment continued day in day out. One day I went to a pharmacy and picked up some needles ready for a chemical or air bubble injection.

On the way home I dropped into a pub for a relaxing pint. Two lads were standing at the bar. One of them pointed me out

"See him over there? You know Alan a fitter who works in installation?"

"Yes" said the other.

"Went to Personnel and says that he wanks." The other laughed so much I thought he was going to burst a blood vessel.

"Well anyway now he says he's going to commit suicide." More hilarity.

By this time it was end of January 1990. I used to carry a needle round as a "friend" ready to use at any time. I thought about it for a few days but there were too many unanswered questions. Why was I being picked on? Were shrinks picking on me? Was it them who were making my life Hell? Were they going to give me the evidence I needed to force a trial? If so, when?. Injection wasn't the answer so I threw the needles away.

In the bar of the Willowbank one day through a doorway I could see two girls talking about me. One of them turned to the other and said "He's not a pervert" shaking her head "It's the stress", her hands indicating a build-up (of stress) in her ribcage. I developed a nervous twitch.

Later another night through the same doorway I noticed two lads talking about my case. One of them was pointing toward the ceiling "The charges against him went all the way up to the top". I already had some idea of this because Lord Pryor had sent his secretary to visit the company. I remember on a number of occasions sitting in the bar of the Willowbank with my head in my hands, my elbows on the table thinking "No more. No more. No more stress."

I was in the Stags Head one night with John Ann-Marie and a few other nurses from the Royal Hospital having a drink. To my side I could see a number of young women talking about me, possibly medical students. The one who was running the conversation was empty-handed making exaggerated gestures about drinking and smoking heavily. The more she went on the more I smoked and the more

I drank. I got drunk "All because he masturbates" she said.

It was about this point that the "whispers" started. I took this as subliminal messaging which of course is absurd. As an example of this I was walking home from work one day and a woman with a push chair was crossing the road in front of me. "He's sly", I only just heard. Did she say that or didn't she?

This treatment continued unabated.

I clearly remember on Feb 14 1990 St Valentines Day, exactly a year since I was interviewed by John Heywood and Brian Stewart to join GPT. There was a party on in the Prince William. I went there with John and Ann-Marie to see a comedian come singer who was the turn for the night. A terrible act but everybody laughed politely and applauded at the right time. During the break when no-one was looking he tapped me on the shoulder. When I turned round he quite clearly mouthed the words "I'd rather commit suicide". Another ruined night which I can still clearly remember.

Another night in the Prince William the bar staff around the same time were talking about me. During the course of the conversation he said "We're trying to help him but he doesn't know it". He was talking to someone at the other side of the bar, who was listening intently and watching me. Just as an experiment I mouthed the words "I'm thinking of writing a letter to the National Press." I quite clearly heard him say" If he does there'll be trouble. Knock him down." So the bar staff did. In style.

Everybody I knew now seemed to be picking on me and I'd had enough. I tried to overdose. I took the following day off work, went to a strange pub on London Road and started to drink heavily while taking Paracetamol. I took them till I felt sick, and reasoned that if I was sick then they wouldn't have the same effect so I cut down on the drink. While I was in there someone else turned up. Possibly a more experienced officer "They reckon he didn't know they were there. Says there's nothing that would suit Liverpool like a gas cloud. He's just a bastard and if he does anything about it we'll shoot him. he's threatening suicide. Look he's doing it now", as I was placing another Paracetamol in my mouth. This went on for a couple of days. On the third day, Wednesday, Quiz night at the Willowbank I met John and Ann-Marie as per usual. A few tables away a group of people were talking and watching ours. As I looked at them one of them placed his hands in the air outlining "Big headlines. Big headlines. Man caught masturbating commits suicide." Just to make sure I got the message he repeated it. "Big headlines. Man caught masturbating commits suicide." I couldn't finish the job off. Not just the fact of my death but the nature of it, and the allegations made against me. My aunt and grandmother lost a cousin of mine due to murder. It destroyed them. I couldn't do that to my mam. Comment to Ann-Marie that night was "They know how to pull strings." After a few more days of treatment Terry Crewe of the A.J. saw what a state I was in and advised me to go to a G.P. By this time I was shaking uncontrollably, whimpering and with a nervous twitch. I didn't have a G.P. in Liverpool and didn't trust the company one who Personnel knew well so I asked

19

Terry for an address. Terry left the pub I think to meet a few friends in CID and later returned with the address of Dr Barnet who was just round the corner from where I lived. I duly visited Dr Barnet who took one look at me and immediately gave me a letter for Sefton General Hospital to see a psychiatrist. I couldn't understand why Sefton General while (I thought) I was being treated by shrinks from the Royal. Still, anyway I took the letter there and later an appointment was made to see a Dr Ferran.

My treatment continued. In the bar of the Prince William two people were standing next to me talking. One said "It's like a broken record. Did he or didn't he? The jury's still out on that one. The majority think he didn't." Later the same person at the same bar on another night said "They're 99% sure he didn't." "Hold on" I thought "In that case they're 99% confident I'm innocent. Why was I still being picked on?" They'd held a trial by applying stress, decided I was innocent yet they were still picking on me. I couldn't understand it.

I later was asked outright by Valerie Crewe of the A.J. "Are they still picking on you?". Was who still picking on me? CID? Personnel? A team of shrinks? No matter who, I confirmed they were. "Yes" I responded "Still picking on me." This formed a bone of contention between Terry and his wife Val. After yet another night of treatment Valerie looked at the state of me and said sympathetically "All because he plays with himself". Another time she complained bitterly to Terry about the treatment I was receiving "Shut up!" shouted Terry across the back of the bar "Shut up! They know what they're doing."

After I received a date for an appointment at hospital I was asked by Terry when it was, so I told him. It was in a few weeks but after this the heavy artillery stepped in.

One of a number of times in the Willowbank "He's a cunt, he's a bastard, he's just a bag of shit, he's an arsehole a wanker a tosser a shithouse shithead smackhead slaphead" more cunts bastards and bags of shit. Some of these came as new insults to me. I later found out from friends what a slaphead and smackhead were. It was the first time I'd heard anybody being called "A bag of shit", but it wasn't the last. One night early during the course of this treatment in the Willowbank someone who I took to be the CID officer who was running the case turned up and explained how he had systematically manufactured evidence. There were two people talking about how he had set about trying to entice me on numerous occasions.

On one occasion with one of the prostitutes "He's that bloody tight he wouldn't even give her a light "I didn't have one. With two other prostitutes "I even paid them to pick him up. He wouldn't even buy them a drink "I had offered to buy the drinks but the barman took her money instead of mine. "He' got a baby girl and he hasn't even bothered to see her." "Eh?" I thought "Even I didn't know that". I later realised that to come to this conclusion I must have been followed home during the previous Christmas holiday and a conversation misinterpreted. The woman was already pregnant when I had sex with her. This appeared to confirm and enhance my belief that I was being followed everywhere I went. Just to reinforce this idea he said "You should hear the radio going Crrr Crrr". He then noticed me observing him and his friend via the bar mirror "Look he's lip-reading us now." I wasn't; I could hear every word he said. Then he pointed someone I noticed and thought might be a shrink looking through the bar hatchway. "You should hear the crap that he's coming out with." the officer said. Ken the landlord later went up to this silver-haired shrink and asked "Did he know they were there?" "No," came the reply "he'd be off", his right hand pointing out that I'd have traveled. True. The investigating officer went on to explain again how he illegally set about gaining and manufacturing evidence while I was in the Derwent Hotel. How he and his friend waited ages and were "Sweating like pigs. We've even got pictures of him. With all the trouble he's caused you'd think he's got a whopper. It's only that big", his fingers indicating the size of my erect penis. "Christ!" I thought." Had they invaded my privacy that far?". Gutted, dirty and cheap is only mild. It was then that I developed a nervous twitch. He concluded "Christ I wish he'd just piss off back to Whitley Bay and toss himself off it. We'll dispirit him."

At about the beginning of May 1989 some people who I took to be students turned up at the Willowbank discussing what was going on

"How many people has it taken so far?" asked one
"One hundred and forty five" replied another.
"How much has it cost?"

"About seventy grand." came the reply "They reckon he's dangerous."

They went on to discuss the case of Georgi Markov a Bulgarian dissident who died after weeks of agony after an irin (sarin? ricin?) injection.

"Christ" was the concluding statement.

By this time it was getting close to my hospital appointment at Sefton General at the psychiatric unit. I was imagining all kinds of horrors. If I was being tormented unofficially by the shrinks then I could only imagine what torture I would endure if they were given unfettered control over me. The answer I concluded was to do something which I had already ruled out as being abhorrent. One night I went up to one of the barmaids of the Willowbank and said

"Guilty."

"What?" she replied.

"Guilty."

"What of masturbating?"

"Yes."

"What in front of young children?"

"Yes."

"Urgh." she commented.

I lied, in style. Somehow they, whoever they were, hadn't just dispirited me, they broke me, both mentally and spiritually. Not because I was guilty of any offence, but because I was innocent. Where this barmaid got her information from I don't know. To this day I still don't believe John or Ann-Marie, by now both trainee nurses, the only people I confided in, would've said anything. The only evidence against me was the say-so of people with a personal grudge. When Ann-Marie heard about this confession the following day she said she didn't care anymore. I believe she was heartily sickened by what she herself had seen of the treatment I was receiving.

Soon after this came Thursday night the day before my hospital appointment when I got a few answers. Two more of the shrinks unofficially treating me turned up at the Willowbank Hotel. They discussed the case in some detail. At first I couldn't hear them properly in the lounge due to other people talking, so I went in the bar. The shrinks followed me.

"He's not a pervert" commented one.

"No" said the other, "A true pervert wouldn't show signs of stress. He didn't know they were there."

"No he sensed a presence."

In my pliable stats of mind I accepted that.

Or was this the last stage in which my mind was distorted?

The conversation continued: "Pity we forced him to admit to it."

"Yes, we forced him to."

"He wanted to improve his own lot."

"Yes even in the afterlife." I'm not a believer in any afterlife.

"Yes a true socialist. He wanted his share. We tried to get him a pension but they wouldn't have it."

"No. Six hundred thousand pounds was too much. We will get him the pension; all he's got to do is take time off sick. They concluded; "Pity we forced him to admit to it, we won't use so much stress next time." And off they went never to be seen again.

The next day I was interviewed at Sefton General Hospital Liverpool in order to be admitted. I was interviewed by a Dr Ferran who was working under the consultant psychiatrist Dr Poole. The first half of the interview was pretty innocuous stuff, personal history, career history, family history etc. However then he asked me what was the problem. I explained that I was being followed everywhere, seemingly watched by everyone I came across and that I was being called all kind of names. At this point he asked if I thought my thoughts were being controlled. I thought the question absurd. After all who better to control your mood or mode of thought than a team of shrinks so I replied in the positive. Then I noticed the term 'delusions'.

I couldn't believe it.

To me a delusion was a hallucination. I have since found out that this is not always so. Dr Ferran at the end explained that he felt I was ill and he wanted to admit me for treatment. At first I was reluctant but when I went outside the stress was maintained so eventually I admitted myself on a voluntary basis as a jelly-legged, thigh rubbing, nervous twitching, and full body shaking, whimpering, and quivering nervous wreck. After I admitted myself to Sefton General Hospital, Wavertree, Liverpool, my recovery from these 'voices' was instantaneous and miraculous. Before any medication was given and even before the alcohol wore off, literally the second I arrived in hospital. The only time in hospital that these delusions recurred was when I phoned work to tell them I was off sick. I was walking out of the ward later when three smartly dressed young gents were walking in. Comment from one of them was "I knew there was something wrong with him all along." Upon my return to the ward I found out that I had been visited by three smartly dressed young gents from the Personnel department at work.

I spent ten weeks in hospital on that occasion recovering from that ordeal and have had numerous admissions into hospital since. These 'delusions' have only ever occurred twice since that admission, once in Liverpool and once in my home city of Sunderland. After ten weeks in hospital I returned to work. I still didn't know the clinical diagnosis of my condition but as soon as I did return the Director of Engineering Personnel was keen to speak to me. He was obviously keen to show me my personnel records. There was nothing incriminating included in them but what was of note was what was missing. My application form, my c.v. my references, photocopies of my Degree and A.C.G.I. my accommodation records. There was quite a lot missing which should have been there. In my fragile state of mind I decided not to say anything at the time and spent my efforts on my recovery. I kept wondering "Why stress?. Why so much stress? Why did they apply so much stress?"

It wasn't until a few months later with my regular hospital visits that I was told by the consultant psychiatrist Doctor Poole that I had been diagnosed with depression that I started wondering instead "How can stress, extremes of stress applied over a period of months actually help someone overcome depression?" No matter how I tried to rationalize it I reasoned that it wouldn't. Was it in order to obtain a confession out of me? No, because they did and that didn't work. They were also disappointed that I did confess outright. Was it some form of retribution? Possibly, but by obtaining a confession in that case I should have been charged. They didn't dare because in that case the way this confession was obtained, under extreme duress would become public knowledge.

It wasn't until a later visit to Sefton General Hospital that Dr Poole clarified that he had diagnosed and was treating me for paranoia, that what happened to me became a lot clearer. I was walking to the bank one lunchtime and asked myself "How can stress help someone with paranoia?" It wouldn't. It was the shrinks treating me originally who were making my life miserable. Dr Poole seemed to know nothing of this, so it was shrinks as Valerie Crewe asked, were picking on me. After I made this determination it took about five seconds for me to realize what happened to me and how. How to commit G.B.H. or murder without breaking the law.

Firstly, you have your victim followed everywhere he or she goes. It's important that your target doesn't see who by, just made to feel ill at ease by sensing that they're being watched. Secondly your target (in my case) goes out drinking every night, so people are positioned around the target (potential victim) to watch and observe everything he or she does. Next you position people around the victim talking about him or her. Generally goading the target and knocking him or her down mentally but basically just taking about them. What you're doing is applying stress, which is a psychiatric tool you need to drive your victim completely 'off their trolley'. Of course if the victim realizes what you're trying to do they might do something about it. Like call in Scotland Yard or the press, so to get round that problem you convince your target and everyone else that you're actually trying to help him or her. To back this idea up the target is given the occasional 'pep talk' and everyone is told that the victim will be made rather wealthy soon. Just to add to the victims' stress and confusion you pick them up on the slightest thing they say or do and make on that they're dangerous and under some form of threat. Maintain the levels of stress constantly for a period of approximately four months and you end up with a deliberately induced severe depression and paranoid schizophrenia. As a course of "treatment" it takes 140-150 or so different people and at the time cost around seventy thousand pounds.

The object of the exercise is that once you've deliberately induced severe mental illness the question becomes at what time did paranoia set in? Was it after being picked on by a team of shrinks for four months? Was it after being picked on by a diagnosed sadist for six months? Was it due to a supposed imaginary conversation across a canteen table? Or did it happen naturally as a result of alcohol abuse? The line adopted by the company, ever since paranoia was diagnosed has been the latter. On the other hand, if my experiences can be proven even in the slightest the question then becomes: who's going to be investigated for attempted murder? It may sound absurd but the fact that I tried to end my life is a perfectly natural and highly predictable reaction to the treatment I received. Four times so far. As such a case, if proven, could be made for not just slander, conspiracy and grievous bodily harm but attempted murder itself. If you try to poison someone then it is an obvious case of attempted murder. However if you poison someones mind to the point of suicide then there is no come-back. Who should be prosecuted for this attempted murder, the Lemos family and a fitter? Gary Head and Personnel at work? Or a team of shrinks and the highest levels of management at GEC, subsequently Marconi?

My delusions only returned once during the rest of my time at Liverpool. After I figured out what had happened to me I waited some time to refer my experiences to Dr Poole, consultant psychiatrist at Sefton General. He dismissed this "conspiracy theory" for two reasons. Firstly, inducing paranoia is recognized as being difficult. My delusions did say that what they're trying to do was quite difficult and not without risk. The risk is you murder your victim during the course of, or after the "treatment". Secondly, medication was not used, which would make the "treatment" quite simple. My delusions did say that they could help me a lot easier if they could prescribe barbituates. I therefore thought about buying them on the black market but in my naivety I didn't know where to go to, who to ask for, what to ask for, how many to take or how much to pay. However as a result of this I have long suspected and only recently in September 2003 confirmed using the internet that the easy way to induce paranoia is to trick your victim into taking barbituates and apply stress. More expert medical and psychiatric knowledge that my supposed imagination gave me. My delusions only returned after I mentioned in passing to John Moss that I was deliberately driven paranoid. My boss Brian suddenly decided to tell me about his brain damaged daughter, possibly as a result of medical negligence. She probably still has the capacities of a six month old baby and will never recover. However he did say that he even considered euthenasia, which would suit everybody.

There he was talking about possibly murdering his own daughter and he previously reckoned I had character problems? Not like that I don't. I pointed out that my personnel files were deficient and in my case the damage was deliberate. He agreed that in that case even he would complain. The following day Lord Pryor head of Marconi turned up at the Microelectronics Centre on a surprise unscheduled visit, looking rather sheepish. Just an impression.

Later that night, with no-one else around, a man sat behind me. "Cunt" he said "Bastard, bag of shit, arse hole (blah blah etc etc)" I took this as a direct threat to start all over again and probably murder me, so I said no more during my time at Liverpool. However I was asked a number of odd questions by John Moss and Brian. Who were my references? Where did I get my Degree? When did I get my Degree? I was curious as to why they asked them. The answer came in August 2002 when I coincidently met one of my references. He asked why, a year or so after I started at Liverpool he was asked for a repeat reference. This beggars the question as to why GPT Personnel would ask for a repeat reference if mine hadn't been "lost" or otherwise destroyed? I suggest they were trying to rebuild their records.

When the redundancies came I was first against the wall.

I returned to my home town, now a city. However my mental illness raises a whole raft of issues which I've racked my damaged brain cell over for years So I'll probably be damned by the public if this account becomes public knowledge but I'll be damned by my own concerns if it doesn't.

The first and most worrying of the issues at stake is that no matter what the rights and wrongs of any individual case, instantly, without any legal, medical or psychiatric knowledge, training or experience I'm supposed to have devised, planned, researched and implemented a ways and means of committing GBH or murder without apparently breaking the law. There is no legal defence against this form of treatment; the only way of avoiding it is not to walk out the door. All the victim would be doing then is adding agoraphobia to a long list of 'symptoms'. If the target succeeds in a suicide attempt then everything points to a suicide while the balance of the mind is disturbed. Nobody ever thinks it may have been deliberately disturbed by a team of shrinks: turns violent and the target is either sectioned or imprisoned. In my case I became a voluntary patient. Trouble is, if the victim doesn't show signs of stress then there's something wrong with them anyway. If the victim tries to make an official complaint then all this would do is to speed up the diagnosis. My own 'symptoms' include: super intelligence, clairvoyance, telekinesis, telepathy and mass hysteria. Let me emphasize that it's not me claiming this, but anyone who dismisses my experiences as delusionary. I don't believe in God, the superhuman or paranormal, so in my eyes my experiences need to be explained rationally. A few years ago I wrote an abbreviated account of events and sent a copy to Liverpools' Chief Constable. The matter was investigated by a Mr Hounsell. I was not involved in the investigation in any way. I was never questioned, interviewed or consulted in any way. To this day I still don't understand how a complaint can be fully investigated without even bothering to assess the full nature of the complaint. The reason for this was on grounds of cost; the cost of a return coach fare from Sunderland to Liverpool, which I'd be quite happy to meet myself. Even a single sentence;

Dear Sir,

Please provide more information.

yours faithfully

would have given me a higher level of confidence that my complaint was taken seriously. After some effort Mr Hounsell wrote to say he couldn't explain my 'symptoms'; super intelligence, clairvoyance etc. This gives me a very low level of confidence that even an attempted murder investigation was taken seriously; it wasn't worth the price of a postage stamp. A report was sent by Mr Hounsell to the Police Complaints Authority, who accepted it. I by law was not privy to that report. However the PCA should have easily seen that the original complaint was not complete, which I expected to make clear at interview. Which raises the question as to whether this intransigence (negligence? collusion?) institutionalized? How often does the PCA turn down a report and why wasn't I interactively involved in the one about my complaint? So I believe the PCA can also be criticized. The next issue raised is the concept of privacy of the individual and the rights of the wrongly accused. My own privacy may or may not have been invaded by a person or persons in the Lemos household. It was nevertheless invaded by the publicity department (Viz?) of a major company.

I believe it was certainly invaded by the investigating officer. As far as the original allegation was concerned there was "No evidence" but just the say-so of someone with an obvious grudge was enough to arouse the homosexual interests of a diagnosed sadist, Gary Head. But why would the investigating officer push his luck and try manufacturing evidence? The answer comes in four parts. Firstly, when I was first interviewed for the Liverpool job that night I was mugged. I tried to report this mugging but was 'fobbed off' by the desk officer: hence the investigating officer wrongly made the determination that I was simply out to cause trouble. Secondly, after weeks, if not months of work what he suddenly got was "Four wanks". Or was this evidence deliberately given? Hence the third part. It comes from a conversation between Ray Ellis and Damien Walker, who ran the analogue section "The local police reckon that he's been taking the piss out of them". "what in his situation", said Damien "he must be sick in the head." Four months later I certainly was "sick in the head". The answer to any possible legal action is to make the victim so "sick in the head" that it takes years to recover, by which time the students have graduated, people have left or simply forgot what happened.

The chances of developing schizophrenia during the course of a lifetime is about 1 in 100. Mine developed during a specific four months so the chances of that is around 1% of 1%. These statistics alone give me 99.99% confidence in my case. Couple that with my other "symptoms" (super intelligence clairvoyance etc) then my "mental illness" becomes no longer a statistical freak. It is as deterministic as DNA, fingerprint or dental records. People have been previously hung or sentenced to life in prison on less. In the fourth part gaining a conviction would justify GPT Personnels' treatment of me.

As far as the rights of privacy and the wrongly accused go, witness John Leslie, a television presenter whose career and reputation, like mine, lies in tatters after being wrongly accused. He would lose all privacy in court and the claims against him were plastered all over the National Press. Look at what happened to Michael Jackson.

Next comes the concept of the privacy of the mind, not the simple concept of physical privacy i.e. having a physical place to hide. I believe my mind has been distorted and twisted not only by Gary Head but a team of shrinks. Not because I was guilty of any offence but because I was innocent and a team of shrinks convinced Marconi management it would be cheaper and easier if everything I said, saw, did, heard or otherwise experienced could be readily dismissed as the rantings of a raving loony. As another example of the concept of this privacy how would you, the reader like to be forced to share your innermost thoughts and feelings with an absolute stranger, even if it is a consultant psychiatrist? I never have enjoyed it. A team of shrinks hid behind this concept of privacy during the course of, and ever since the "treatment" they gave me. Which leads me to the real reason why I tried to confess to the offence: I didn't want to give a team of shrinks the professional (sadistic? psychopathic? homosexually perverted?) gratification of having me calculated to the finest degree.

As far as the treatment is concerned it is clearly a serious sex offence not by me but against me. The more serious part of it is the homosexual gratification obtained by controlling the victims mind and behavior. I'd rather have confessed to killing my own grandmother, but they did get a confession out of me. In my eyes no matter how ill I was (seriously ill) that does make me all the "cunts bastards and bags of shit" under the Sun. I have seen other cases in hospital where the mental damage done far outweighs the physical but because mental illness is involved it is not taken seriously.

How about the rights of the mentally ill? Because mental illness is involved everything I say and do can be simply ignored, as has happened in the past. I previously tried to get in touch with someone from GPT Personnel who did work for the Samaritans, possibly the person who "Knew there was something wrong with him all along."

As such even Liverpool Samaritans refused to help.

A double bind situation can be typified by a contradictory statement or group of statements. It can be simplified by a simple sentence

"Every sentence I say is a lie"

If that is a lie then you are telling the truth so you are lying and so on. According to the classical model a single double bind situation is enough to cause schizophrenia. At the last count I was caught in about eight; for example I wanted a court case but didn't want the accompanying publicity. That gives the reader some idea as to how distorted my mind has been for the past 20 or more years. I will probably never recover: the end at least of my career for telling one man a simple crude joke.

Under law, in theory, I could be forcibly lobotomised just on the say-so of two malevolent medicians, which would guarantee the destruction of all evidence which I may have between my ears. Even ECT would have had a similar effect. So by definition of the offence a team of shrinks get away with what they were up to, which is the whole object of their work anyway. Last, and I've now decided least, of the topics my mental illness raises is a lesson in economics theory: how a single person with an obvious grudge can be blown out of all proportion into having major ramifications. I estimate my redundancy cost the company? 35-50 million in lost throughput and potential cost savings. This may sound grandiose but three months part time effort, about 80 hrs full time work saved the company an estimated #15 million over three years. It'd take two years to train up a replacement so #35-50 m may be reasonable. However what I believe came to light at this "High powered meeting about a pain up the 'arris" was the systematic destruction of the companys' managerial structure using the judicial system. This managerial structure was used to spread rumour, innuendo and lies by the then Director of Personnel. That could be the true cost of my own mental illness, perhaps even the loss of Diretoral leadership with the potential loss of the site and about 2000 jobs. As a result of that possibility it wouldn't surprise me if the highest levels of management, not only of GPT but of Liverpool Constabulary were directly involved. However, like I said that is the least of the issues raised; the main one requiring changes or clarification in law, which is over and above the average Chief Constable. Other points may need procedural changes or changes in public perception. As a result I believe the implications involved do require close scrutiny, and this alone does justify reiterating my complaint.

The point behind publishing this article is that if a victims' schizophrenia can be shown to be caused by an act of malice then it is pensionable. The victim may never work again, will probably spend years in and out of hospital and will never reach full potential due to lost time off work and lost promotion and job prospects. Even if it only applies to 1 case in 1000 of schizophrenics that is 2500 people in the US alone. At 3-5 million dollars per pension for the average 30-year old, you do the maths at what the above may mean to victims.

Appendix

I have long been of the firm belief that I wasn't the first or last person to receive this form of "treatment". On December 2009 I went into Google and typed in "Marconi employee suicide" in the search rules and a number of suspicious deaths turned up. The authorities claim that these 22 deaths are not statistically significant as the company employed 50,000 people. However all these suspicious deaths were of highly intelligent highly trained personnel working on specific projects at a technical level. I estimate that there could only be about 100-150 people working at that level on those projects at that time. That is a death rate of about 16-22%, eight to ten times higher than front line troops being shot at or blown up in Afghanistan. The general public have been given the "mushroom treatment" (kept in the dark and fed with something rather unpleasant). The deaths outlined by Computer News are summarized below:-

Professor Keith Bowden	fatal car crash	verdict accident
Lt Colonel Anthony Godley	mysterious disappearance	Presumed dead
Roger Hill	shotgun blast	verdict suicide
Jonathan Walsh	fell from building	verdict open
Vimal Dajibhai	drove off bridge	verdict open
Arshad Sharif	self decapitation	verdict suicide
Richard Pugh	suffocation	verdict accident

Dr John Brittan	carbon monoxide poisoning	verdict accident
David Skeels	carbon monoxide poisoning	verdict open
Victor Moore	drug overdose	verdict suicide
Peter Peapell	carbon monoxide poisoning	verdict open
David Sands	car crash	verdict open
Stuart Gooding	car crash	verdict accident
George Kountis	drowning	verdict misadventure
Shani Warren	drowning verdict open	
Mark Wisner	suffocation	verdict open
Michael Baker	car crash verdict	misadventure
Russell Smith	fall from cliff	verdict suicide
Trevor Knight	carbon monoxide poisoning	verdict suicide
Alistair Beckham	electrocution	verdict open
Peter Ferry	electrocution	verdict open
Andrew Hall	carbon monoxide poisoning	verdict suicide

My own experiences with Marconi puts each of these suspicious deaths into a completely different perspective. There may be other survivors of the way I was treated: like me seriously mentally ill but they may not realize how. What I believe is required is the formation of a pressure group; I have invested considerable effort in trying to obtain a criminal investigation into my own case but there are other people involved not just myself.